Jesus and the breakfast barbecue

by Diane Walker

Silence, except for the swishing of the water.

Darkness, except for the few lights
still lit in the village.

The fishermen weren't working yet that night. But one of them was there on the beach.

It was Peter. He leant against the side of his boat, where it rested safely on the pebbly shore. He felt very alone.

He was thinking about another time he had felt so alone, just a few nights ago. Peter and the other disciples had shared a special meal with Jesus. They had all been upset when Jesus said they would all leave him later that night.

"I won't leave you, Jesus," Peter had replied immediately, "no matter how dangerous it is!"

Now he remembered how Jesus had looked at him as he said, "Peter, before you hear the cockerel crowing in the morning, you will say three times that you do not even know me."

Soon afterwards, in a quiet garden, soldiers arrested Jesus, and took him away to be tried. Just as Jesus had said, the disciples ran away – all except Peter.

Peter crept along behind the soldiers, making sure they couldn't see him. They took Jesus to a house for questioning. Others gathered round the fire in the yard outside, warming their hands. But Peter skulked in the shadows, cold and lonely.

But people recognised him. Peter was terrified: perhaps they would arrest him, too! Three times he said he did not even know Jesus – then he heard the cockerel crowing, and he realised what he had done.

Peter didn't like to think about the time following Jesus' arrest. But his mind kept going back to it, worrying at it, just as your tongue goes back to a wobbly tooth, no matter how many times you try to stop it.

Jesus' enemies found him guilty, even though he had done nothing wrong.

They killed him.

Some of the disciples watched as he died. They watched as his body was laid in a burial cave.

They could hardly believe what was happening. Jesus – their friend, the Teacher, the Healer, the man they had believed was special – was dead. They were alone. They were all heartbroken. Peter felt guilty as well. He was ashamed of the way he had treated Jesus.

They all thought that their friendship with Jesus was over. But then – suddenly, amazingly, miraculously – they saw Jesus again! He was alive!

All the other disciples looked forward to the next time they saw Jesus, but Peter felt worse and worse. Jesus knew this, and came to see him so the two of them could talk alone.

Now in the quiet night, Peter wrapped his cloak more tightly around him, and gazed out at the moontrack on the lake. Once, Jesus had told him that he had a special job for him to do. But he knew that that was all over. So here he was, sitting on the beach alone, not knowing what to do next.

“I’m useless!” he whispered to himself. “I couldn’t even admit I knew him. How can he even bear to be friends with me now?”

Thinking of what he had thrown away, Peter buried his head in his arms, and began to cry.

He could hear voices. Some men were coming: it was about time for the fishing boats to set off. Hurriedly, Peter dried his eyes, rubbing them roughly on his cloak. He stood up. Some of the other disciples were there with the fishermen.

"I'm going fishing, too!" Peter shouted. "Anyone going to join me?"

Several of them agreed. Shouting and laughing as John skidded in the pebbles, they loaded the nets, pushed the boat out, and jumped in.

James and Thomas took the oars, and pulling strongly, they were soon in position. They threw the net over the sides and settled down to wait.

No one spoke to Peter. They knew something was wrong with him. But they realised he didn't want to talk, and kept quiet.

"They know what I did," Peter thought "They don't even want to speak to me." And he looked away to hide his face.

The hours passed. They drew up the net, moved on and recast, but they caught nothing.

Gradually, the sky lightened. The sun showed itself above the hills, and warm, golden light streaked across the water. Nathanael stood up and stretched. "It's time to give in," he said. "Come on, let's go home for breakfast."

Drawing in the net, they set off for the shore. And then James pointed ahead. "Look," he said, "there's someone on the beach."

Shading their eyes against the sun, they watched the man as they drew nearer to the shore.

Then they heard him shout, “Have you caught any fish?”

They shouted back, “Not even one!”

“Throw your net out over the other side of the boat!” the man answered.

They looked at each other and shrugged. It wasn’t likely they would suddenly catch anything, but they had nothing to lose.

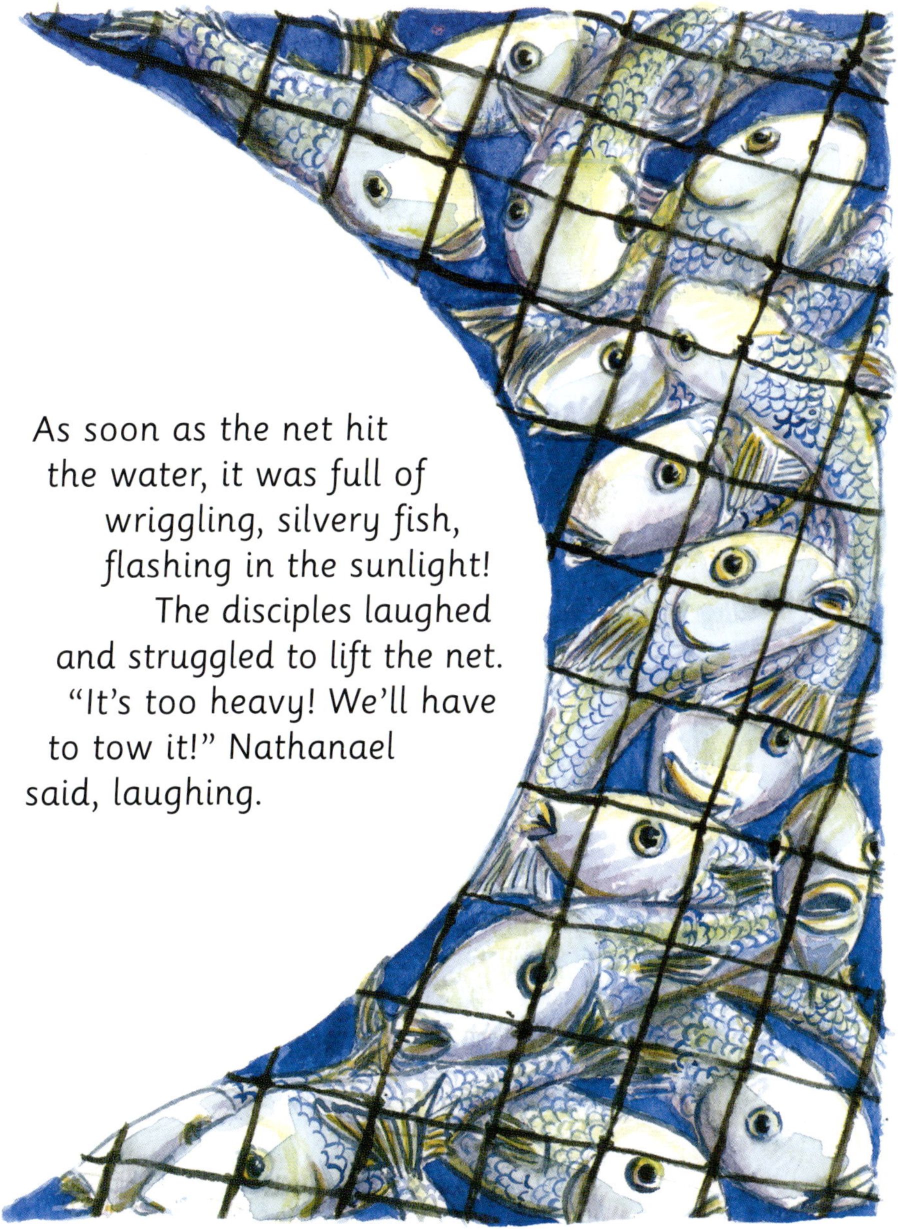

As soon as the net hit the water, it was full of wriggling, silvery fish, flashing in the sunlight! The disciples laughed and struggled to lift the net. "It's too heavy! We'll have to tow it!" Nathanael said, laughing.

"It's Jesus!" John shouted.
Peter looked at the man on the shore. Suddenly, he knew he had to be with Jesus straight away. He wrapped his cloak round him, leapt into the water and waded ashore.

"You've worked hard tonight," Jesus said to them when the others arrived. "What about some breakfast?"

There, on a fire built in a nest of pebbles, was some fish and freshly baked bread. They smelt appetising to the hungry men, and soon they were all enjoying the unexpected meal.

There was plenty for everyone. After that they lay back, gazing at the clouds as they drifted across the morning sky. Soon, they would carry the fish up to the market in the town. But now it was a time for being quiet, and for remembering other meals they had shared like this through the years.

Jesus stood up, and asked Peter to go with him. The two of them walked along the beach, the pebbles clinking under their feet.

They could hear voices from the town, as the market began. Ahead of them, two children ran down to play at the water's edge, scooping water into the old pots they had brought.

Jesus watched them, smiling. “Peter,” he said, “do you love me?”

Peter stopped, shocked, and looked at him. Didn’t Jesus know how he felt, how sorry he was for letting him down?

Didn’t he know that he longed more than anything to make things all right again between them?

“Lord,” he said, “you know I love you.”

Jesus nodded. “Then look after my people,” he said.

Jesus asked the same question twice more, and twice more Peter tried to tell him how he felt. And twice more Jesus asked Peter to look after his people.

Then Peter remembered how he had said three times that he didn't know Jesus. He realised that Jesus was showing him that he had cancelled out what he had done: three failures, three new chances to get things right. And this time, Jesus believed that Peter would get it right! He trusts me, Peter thought. He trusts me to do this job for him. He really has forgiven me. This is a new start.

Peter looked out over the shore: at the children playing in the water as it was turned into liquid gold by the sun and at the other disciples as they lay relaxing before the day's work.

It was the start of a new day.